24 CHRISTMAS STORIES

Faith and Traditions from Around the World

WRITTEN BY JUDITH BOUILLOC

ILLUSTRATED BY MADELEINE BRUNELET, CLAIRE DELVAUX, MIZUHO FUJISAWA, CÉCILE GUINEMENT, CLÉMENCE MEYNET, AGNÈS PERRUCHON, AND BRUNO ROBERT

TRANSLATED BY GRACE MCQUILLAN

Sky Pony Press
New York

10 9 8 7 6 5 4 3 2 1

Manufactured in China, April 2023
This product conforms to CPSIA 2008

Library of Congress Cataloging-in-Publication Data is available on file.

Cover design by Fabrice Mauer & Kai Texel
Cover illustrations by Madeleine Brunelet
Back cover illustration by Bruno Robert
Text by Judith Bouilloc
Illustrations by Madeleine Brunelet, Claire Delvaux, Mizuho Fujisawa, Cécile Guinement, Clémence Meynet, Agnès Perruchon, Bruno Robert
French editorial direction by Isabelle de Wulf
US Edition edited by Nicole Frail

Print ISBN: 978-1-5107-7607-4
Ebook ISBN: 978-1-5107-7608-1

For Rita, Juliette, and Joachim
Diane and Alyssa
Noémie, Aymeric, and Sylvia

Table of Contents

It's Advent!

Anna opens the first window of her Advent calendar.

"Papa, is Christmas here yet?"

"No, today is the first day of Advent."

"What's Advent?" Anna asks, counting the squares on the calendar.

"The word Advent means 'arrival' or 'coming,'" says Papa.

"Who's coming?"

"Jesus is coming."

Anna makes an Advent wreath out of pine tree branches and big gold bows. She places four red candles in it to symbolize hope, peace, joy, and love.

Every Sunday, Papa lights a new candle.

There is more and more light.

"Is it almost Christmas?"

"Be patient, Anna."

Anna walks in the snow. She arranges the figurines in her nativity scene and decorates the Christmas tree. Every day she asks, "Is it Christmas? Is Jesus coming?"

"Not yet."

The little girl hangs one red stocking and one green stocking above the fireplace. She watches the last of the autumn leaves fly away outside the window.

"Is it Christmas? Is Jesus coming?"

Her mother reads her a story every night. A story to prepare her heart.

"Is it Christmas?"

Anna waits and whispers, "Come, Lord Jesus, come!"

How to Make Bredele with a Baby Dragon

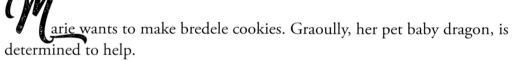

Marie wants to make bredele cookies. Graoully, her pet baby dragon, is determined to help.

"What are bredele, anyway?" he asks, flying over the table.

"Bredele are the butter cookies we always bake during Advent. They're an Alsatian specialty," the little girl explains. "There are all kinds of different ways to make them, but today we're going to make zimtsterne, or cinnamon stars."

Graoully claps his paws together. He can't wait to make bredele.

"Go ahead, Graoully! Pour the flour in the bowl."

The baby dragon dumps the whole bag in at once.

"Uh oh! That's way too much!"

Graoully scoops out the extra flour with one of his paws. Then Marie adds ground almonds, sugar, and cinnamon to the bowl.

"Now we have to crack the eggs, separate the whites from the yolks, and add the egg yolks to the dough."

Graoully squeezes an egg over the bowl . . . and the yolk, full of pieces of crushed eggshell, drips down from between his claws.

"Not like that, Graoully! You have to be gentle."

The baby dragon tries cracking another egg but only manages to smash it on the table.

"Maybe I should be in charge of the eggs," Marie says. "You can do the stirring."

Graoully juggles the wooden spoons while Marie expertly cracks the eggs into the bowl.

"There! I cracked the eggs," she announces. "Now you can mix everything together! But be careful. . . ."

Graoully stirs very carefully and every now and then he takes a break to taste the cookie dough!

"Go faster . . . you're stirring too slowly!"

Graoully churns the spoon so quickly that the bowl shoots up to the ceiling.

"You have to hold onto the bowl," Marie sighs as she looks at the splatters of cookie dough on the walls.

"Oh well, that's okay!" she finally says. "We'll just clean it up later. But we do have to start all over. I'll make the dough and you can make the icing. Just use the electric mixer to beat the egg whites."

Graoully feels a little embarrassed about ruining everything. This time he'll follow Marie's instructions.

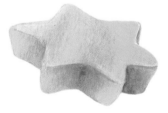

"Look at my egg whites!" he proudly exclaims after a few minutes.

Graoully has beaten the egg whites so thoroughly that the mixture resembles a little mountain of snow.

"Great job, Graoully!"

The little girl sprinkles powdered sugar over the egg whites and stirs the mixture.

Next, Marie rolls out the cinnamon cookie dough while Graoully uses a star-shaped cookie cutter. He cuts out dozens and dozens of cookies.

"Wow!" the young chef says. "Our table looks like the Milky Way!"

Graoully coats the stars in icing and gobbles up two or three in the process.

"Graoully, we have to bake the zimtsterne before we eat them!"

Unfortunately, there's one small problem: the oven simply will not turn on.

"It's broken," Marie moans. "What are we going to do?"

Graoully grabs the tray of cookies, takes a deep breath, and blows out a long burst of flames.

A few of the bredele cookies are a little scorched, but most of them look delicious and smell delightfully of cinnamon.

Graoully licks his chops.

"All right, now you can try them. But please don't eat them all! Bon appétit, Graoully!"

The Carp in the Bathtub

It's been several days since we stopped taking baths in our house. We've been showering at our neighbor's house instead. Why? Because of the carp swimming in our bathtub. We ordered it from the fishmonger. That's what we do in Poland—every year we have carp for Wigilia.* Grandmother told me that when she was a child, it was very difficult to find fish to eat. So, to make sure there would be carp for Christmas Eve, people would buy one as early as they could and then keep it alive in their bathtubs. In our house, we still follow this tradition.

My little brother Karl likes to check on our carp every five minutes. He loves petting it and making sure it has everything it needs. He even gave it a nickname: G, which is short for Gwiazdka, the first star that appears in the sky on Christmas Eve. Once that star comes out, we can sit down and eat. This is why it's so important to always be on the lookout for Gwiazdka!

Unfortunately, I don't think Karl realizes that we are going to eat the carp in a few hours. When Mom asks us if we want it fried, jellied, or with a sauce, he looks horrified.

* Polish Christmas Eve dinner.

"No way, Stan, we can't eat G!" he says, his eyes pleading with me.

He looks so sad that I give in.

"Okay, okay . . ."

And so we've decided to launch a rescue mission to save G, the Christmas carp.

Karl goes to the kitchen to help Mom make oplatek, the unleavened wafer that we'll share tonight when we wish each other Merry Christmas. My little brother intentionally makes a cloud of flour big enough to fill the whole room. While he's distracting Mom, I sneak a plastic bag out of the cupboard.

Our mission has begun! The hardest part now is catching G and getting her into the bag filled with water. When Karl is finally done in the kitchen, he comes to help me. He places his hand flat under the carp's belly, and in a single swoop, he throws her in the bag. Phew. At least the fish doesn't seem to mind being taken for a walk.

We race out of the apartment and tell Mom that we're going to take a shower at the neighbor's.

"All right, boys! Make sure you look nice for tonight!" she shouts from the kitchen. I wink at Karl and we both explode with silent laughter.

We slide down the stairs and head for the pond behind the hill. Karl runs down the street laughing at the top of his lungs. I ask him to be a little more discreet. Shhh! We don't want anyone to see us. After all, we've just committed a kidnapping. And G hasn't made it to safety yet.

After walking for a few minutes, we arrive at the pond. The surface of the water is calm and partly frozen. I'm so mesmerized by how beautiful it looks that I don't notice what's under my feet. I slip on the muddy ground and land face down in the slush. "Some rescuer you are!" Karl chuckles as he gives me his hand. Lucky for us, he's the one carrying the bag with G in it. And he was certainly being more careful than I was. He even remembered to put on his boots!

Karl wades into the water and says his goodbyes to G. He releases the fish from her plastic bubble, and together we watch as she wriggles and swims away before disappearing in the pond like a shadow.

"Now she's free!" Karl says happily.

But I can't help thinking that we've just said farewell to tonight's traditional Christmas Eve dinner. My little brother can read my mind and pats me on the shoulder.

"Don't worry. Mom's making mushroom pierogi, soup, poppy seed roll, gingerbread, and tons of other delicious stuff."

I look at him and notice that he has flour in his hair. And my pants are covered in mud.

"Well, I guess we'll have to take that shower at the neighbor's after all."

"No, we won't!" Karl says. "The bathtub's empty!"

December 4
Lebanon

Saint Barbara's Wheat

Village of Maghdouché, southern Lebanon
The night before December 4, the Feast of Saint Barbara

Just like all of the other children in the village, Peter comes home after school and puts on a costume. His sister Nora is letting him borrow her clothes to dress up as Saint Barbara. He's wearing a long blond wig and a blue dress. Nora bursts out laughing when she sees him.

"Wow, some Barbara you are!"

"Well, you don't exactly look like a unicorn!"

Smiling, Nora attaches a gold horn to her forehead and a multicolored mane to her back.

From their house's rooftop terrace, the two children can see fields of carob trees, vineyards, the great city of Saida, and the sea in the distance. At the moment, though, they're not interested in the landscape. They're watching the village streets for any sign of their four friends.

"Look! Charlie's dressed up like a grandma and Nicole is a pineapple!"

Their cousin Charlie does appear to have borrowed his grandmother's cane. He's walking bent at the waist with an old headscarf knotted under his chin. Behind him, Sarah is wearing a crown of braided wheat stalks on her head. She has ten bracelets on each wrist and is sporting traditional Lebanese makeup.

John is a superhero and looks very proud of his red cape blowing in the wind.

The youngest in the group, five-year-old Nicole, is skipping along with the others in her giant pineapple costume.

The six children meet at Nora and Peter's house, and when everyone is ready, they leave together to walk around the village. They knock gleefully on their neighbors' doors. As soon as each door opens, they sing Saint Barbara's song as loudly as they can:

Hechlé Barbara	*Barbara is running away*
Mah banat el hara	*with the girls from the village,*
Hrifta min hinayha	*I recognized her eyes,*
Min lamsit idayha	*the touch of her hand,*
W min hakil ouswara	*and her bracelet*

To thank them for their visit, the villagers give them sweets and a little money. After an hour of knocking and singing, they already have plenty of treats.

"We've gone to all the houses on the street. Where should we go now?" Nora asks.

"How about Uncle Michael's?" Peter replies.

"Oh no, not Uncle Michael," John protests. "He never gives out anything!"

"Let's go to Aunt Roseanne's house," Nicole says. "She's so nice. I'm sure she's going to love my pineapple costume."

The older children agree to this idea and head for their aunt's house. On the way, they pass the statue of Our Lady of Mantara. When they arrive at the house, they knock on the door and sing just as loudly as before, but no one comes to open it.

"Maybe she can't hear us because she's deaf," Nicole says.

"She is? You should have said so!" Sarah sighs and turns the doorknob herself.

The children walk inside and find Roseanne in the kitchen making kamhiyeh for tomorrow's festivities. Kamhiyeh is a dessert made from boiled and sweetened grains of wheat mixed with grated coconut and flavored with anise. It's the traditional dish of Saint Barbara's feast day.

When she sees the six children standing in her kitchen, Aunt Roseanne sprinkles almonds, raisins, and pistachios over the dish and hurries to prepare a bowl for each of them. When that's done, she fills their baskets to the brim with sweets. The children want to thank Roseanne, but she can't hear their singing. Instead, Nicole decides to improvise with a special dance. Roseanne is delighted. It certainly isn't every day that she has a giant pineapple performing in her kitchen!

"We have enough candies to last for at least ten years!" Nora exclaims as the little group walks back out onto the street.

"I'm so thirsty," Charlie grumbles.

"I told you not to eat so much candy!" says Sarah.

"I'm thirsty, too," Nicole whines.

Peter decides to knock on the village priest's door.

"Abouna! Abouna! We're thirsty!" the children cry.

A long gray beard appears in the doorway.

"Come in, you band of rascals," the old priest and owner of the beard mutters. "I'll make some mint tea."

Abouna welcomes the children inside and invites them to sit in the living room.

"Now, children," he says, smoothing his beard. "You know the legend of Saint Barbara, I hope?"

"She was the daughter of a very powerful and very evil man," Peter begins.

"And when he found out that she had converted to Christianity, he was so furious that he locked her in a tower!" Sarah adds.

Charlie wants to tell the next part of the story.

"But Barbara refused to give up her faith, which angered her father more. She fled through the streets of her village to escape him," he says. "And she plastered her face with soot so no one would recognize her," Peter says solemnly.

"No she didn't, she wore a disguise," Nora corrects him.

"A pineapple disguise!" Nicole squeals.

Abouna laughs quietly while he heats the water for tea.

"Don't be silly," Sarah says, showing off her own costume. "She wore a crown of wheat on her head and put on lots of bracelets, just like me."

Charlie vehemently shakes his head and tells yet another version of the story:

"That's not what happened at all! She was running through a field of wheat and the wheat grew while she was running to hide her from the people chasing her. That's why we eat kamhiyeh and sow wheat in our saucers on December fourth. To remember the miracle!"

The old priest clears his throat.

"In the early days of the Church, many Christians died as martyrs, like Saint Barbara. The word 'martyr' means 'witness.' That young Christian woman gave her life to bear witness to her faith. As far as the rest of the story, there are many different versions. Which one of them is true? I haven't the slightest idea. But in my favorite telling of the tale, the story goes that when Saint Barbara was executed, no one knew who she was. People knew nothing about her except that she was a Christian and that she had refused to give up her faith. According to this version of the story, she was an unnamed martyr that people later started calling Barbare because she had been a foreigner. When we celebrate Saint Barbara, who is the patron saint of mineworkers, firefighters, and members of the military, we are also celebrating all of the other forgotten saints and all of the Christians who are still persecuted and overlooked today. All of the heroes for God's love that no one talks about."

John, who hasn't said anything yet, shows the priest his cape.

"It's true," he says. "There are so many unknown heroes. I think it's really sad."

The other children look at the little boy in his superhero costume and try to muffle their laughter. Abouna pours the tea. It smells like the orange blossoms of Maghdouché.

December 5
Belgium

The Christmas Truce

December 24, 1914
Ypres Front Line, Belgium

Here in the trenches, any hope of a short war is long gone. For five months, Lieutenant Willems has watched as bombing and flooding have disfigured his homeland.

The lieutenant looks at the shivering men around him . . . the soldiers he is meant to lead into battle. On this Christmas Eve, they seem more tired of the war than ever.

Lieutenant Willems thinks about the damp that seems to invade everything, about the endless mud that wears down even the strongest souls. He thinks of the men he has lost and the ones he has yet to lose.

To warm his heart, he pictures the blazing fire that at this very moment is lighting up the house he left behind last summer. He thinks about his wife, so courageous, so sweet, and his darling daughters, who have probably put a photo of him on the mantelpiece. They're the ones he's fighting for.

In a few minutes, a French military chaplain will be performing a Christmas mass in the trenches. Willems builds a makeshift altar by flipping over a box of ammunition. One of his corporals adds two candles, each one stands tall in a glass bottle. All but a few of the soldiers gather around, and the priest hands out tiny pieces of communion wafers so that as many people as possible can receive the host.

After the mass, Willems's men make a table near a first aid station out of three rotted wooden planks. They use a tent cover as a tablecloth. The lieutenant invites the wounded poilus from the 16th Battalion of Light Infantrymen to join them. Most of these French soldiers are just ordinary guys from Nord-Pas-de-Calais, but his infantry section fought with them at the Battle of Ramskapelle, and he's seen for himself what incredible fighters these foot soldiers are. In fact, he owes a few of them his life. Willems also invites the Tommies to his improvised Christmas Eve festivities. "Tommies" are what they call the British soldiers. Some of them are Indians wearing turbans and others are Scotsmen wearing kilts.

The wine at this cosmopolitan meal tastes like a mop and the beans taste, well, like beans. The coffee lives up to its nickname ("sock juice"), but there is also good Belgian ale, chocolate and pâté from the French soldiers, and Christmas pudding and whiskey offered by the English. They spend a wonderful evening together, but Willems eventually has to leave them to return to his post.

Around midnight, he looks up at the sky. The clouds have disappeared, and the heavens look calmer and more immense than ever. He would like to say a prayer, to believe in the miracle of Christmas. Today no shots were fired. Tiny snowflakes fall silently. The officer savors this moment of peace.

Stille Nacht, Heilige Nacht!
Alles schläft; einsam wacht
Nur das traute heilige Paar.
Holder Knabe im lockigen Haar,
Schlaf in himmlischer Ruh!
Schlaf in himmlischer Ruh!

A German soldier is singing. He sounds so close. Willems realizes for perhaps the first time that the enemy trench is only a few yards from his own. When the German hymn ends, a voice answers back in French:

Douce nuit, sainte nuit !
Dans les cieux ! L'astre luit.
Le mystère annoncé s'accomplit.
Cet enfant sur la paille endormi, c'est l'amour infini !

The same melody, the same song. "Silent Night." The same faith being spoken from two sides of the battlefield.

When the singing is over, one of the Tommies shouts, "Look! Christmas trees!"

Lieutenant Willems peers at the trench through a firing hole. In place of their machine guns, the Germans have lined up Christmas trees, lanterns, and candles. The French soldiers start singing "Mon Beau Sapin" and the Germans respond with "O Tannenbaum." A Scottish soldier plays the bagpipes. What a strange night.

"Kameraden, Kameraden . . ."

The German voices are getting even closer now. Lieutenant Willems can't believe his eyes. The enemy soldiers are coming out of the trenches waving white handkerchiefs. They're walking unarmed in the middle of no man's land.

Willems's men look at each other. "What should we do, Lieutenant?" their faces seem to say. Willems thinks quickly. They're not supposed to fraternize with their enemies.

But tonight is Christmas. So he nods, and in a firm voice says, "Let's go."

His whole section stands up in a single movement, just like when he gives the order to attack. But instead of his pistol, Willems is carrying a bottle of the best Belgian ale and two glasses!

He walks ahead of his men across the thin layer of newly fallen snow that covers their battleground. What is happening to him is simply not real. He knows this. He can feel it.

In the middle of no man's land, a German officer offers him a warm handshake and a few words. His name is George. He comes from Bavaria. He has two daughters, like Willems. The two officers share a toast.

A few yards away, sausages and chocolates are being thrown over the barbed wire. They make and trade beverages with one another. Men are singing and, for a few hours, everyone forgets that they're at war with one another.

The next morning, the soldiers in spiked helmets stand side by side with the soldiers in berets to pose for photographs. There is even a game of soccer. England versus Germany. They use an old military cap as a ball. The officers in charge observe the scene.

"They look like happy children," the Bavarian says.

"If only wars could be decided on the soccer field," Willems replies.

"England would win every time!" the English captain from Manchester crows.

The three soldiers look at each other and all burst into hearty laughter.

In the mid-afternoon, the Belgian lieutenant calls his soldiers together. He has received furious orders from his superiors. It's time for them to bury themselves in the trench again and get back to fighting a war. It's time to forget about this break from it all . . . this dream. But Lieutenant Willems will never forget. Ever. This truce in 1914 is what will give him the strength to believe that one day the war will end.

A Show for Saint Nicolas Day

December sixth!

Today is Saint Nicolas Day, and Rita is jumping for joy. In her village in the Lorraine region, this is a very special day. Saint Nicolas is coming to her school! He's going to give little presents to all the children who have been good, and Father Fouettard will hand out moldy potatoes to any naughty ones. Last year, everyone in the whole school got chocolates from Saint Nicolas and Father Fouettard had to keep all of his moldy potatoes for himself!

Before she leaves for school, Rita puts a carrot in her backpack. She explains to her mother that it's for Saint Nicolas's donkey. Saint Nicolas never goes anywhere without his donkey. Rita hopes her teacher will let it inside the classroom.

At school, the children start the day by singing the songs they've learned with Miss Juliette:

"Venez! Venez saint Nicolas! Et tralala!"

Miss Juliette claps her hands to help them keep the beat. The students sing as loud as they can so Nicolas will know to hurry up. . . .

"Ô grand Saint Nicolas patron des écoliers
Apporte-moi des pommes dans mon petit panier . . ."

After the singing, the six-year-old students get ready to perform their play about the story of Saint Nicolas. Rita will be playing the role of the third child, and she can't wait!

Her teacher asks everyone to be quiet. The show is starting!

Hans, Emery, and Rita go to harvest wheat in the fields and pick up the stalks of wheat their teacher has placed on the floor. Then they get lost in the forest that the other students built for them out of pine tree branches.

The three children knock on the door of the butcher's shop. The butcher is really just a ten-year-old in a costume, but he still looks really, really scary! At first, he pretends to be nice to Rita, Hans, and Emery and they walk happily inside. The evil butcher lets out a cruel laugh and tosses the three schoolchildren into a large box. It's a salting tub—a huge chest for storing salted meat! The butcher intends to keep the children inside it for seven years!

In real life, though, only thirty seconds go by before Saint Nicolas appears in the classroom. He's wearing his big red coat, his miter, and is carrying his cross. Rita pokes her head out of the box to see him. He's so handsome! But then Emery and Hans start tugging on Rita's sleeve.

"Rita, get back in here. We're supposed to be in the box!"

Saint Nicolas decides to visit the evil butcher and asks for something to eat.

"Would you like a piece of ham?" The villain hands him a slice over the counter.

"No, thank you. It's not very good," Saint Nicolas replies.

"Would you like a piece of veal?"

"No, thank you. It doesn't look very appetizing!"

"You sure are hard to please, Saint Nicolas!" the butcher growls. "What do you want to eat?"

"Salted meat! The meat that's been in your salting tub for seven years!"

When the butcher hears these words, he flees.

"BOOOOOOOO!" the young spectators shout as he hurries offstage.

"Butcher, butcher, don't run away," Saint Nicolas calls after him. "Repent, and God will forgive you."

In her hiding place, Rita holds her breath. This is her favorite part. Saint Nicolas stretches out three fingers over the box. Then Hans jumps up out of it!

He stretches and yawns. "I slept so well!"

Then it's Emery's turn. "So did I!"

Then Rita pops out and cries, "I thought I was in heaven!"

SALTING TUB

The three children wrap Saint Nicolas in an enormous hug. They have been brought back to life and the play is over! The room fills with loud applause and their teacher congratulates her young actors.

Now Saint Nicolas can start handing out his treats. This year he gives the children clementines, chocolate, and gingerbread with his picture on it!

"Thank you, Saint Nicolas!" says Rita.

Father Fouettard, who arrived late, tries to start a frowning contest. But nothing he does can change the fact that Saint Nicolas is the star of the day. All of the students want to touch him and talk to him.

"Where did you leave your donkey?" Emery asks.

"On the playground."

"What's his name?"

"Velvet. Because he's very soft."

"Teacher, teacher, can we go see Velvet?"

"Yes, it's time to go outside!" says Miss Juliette.

"Yippee! I can give him my carrot!" Rita squeals.

The students rush to the playground to say hello to Velvet, leaving Saint Nicolas behind.

"Well, well . . . it looks like Velvet is more popular than I am! I guess no one can compete with a donkey," he sighs.

But not all of the children have left. Emery is still in the classroom and he would very much like to ask Saint Nicolas a few questions.

"Great Saint Nicolas, was that a true story? Did you really save three children after they'd been trapped by an evil butcher?"

"Not exactly. I'll tell you the original story. In the fourth century, there were three valiant soldiers who were unjustly accused of plotting against the emperor. Those three warriors were imprisoned and sentenced to death for a crime they hadn't committed."

"That's terrible!"

"Luckily, I convinced the emperor that they were innocent. And the emperor granted them their freedom!"

"Wow!"

"As the centuries passed, the three innocent soldiers in the story became three little children, their prison tower became a salting tub, and their freedom became a resurrection."

"And that's how the story became a legend!"

"Exactly!" Saint Nicolas says, taking off his hat.

"I really like your funny hat!" Emery says.

"This isn't a hat, it's a miter! It's the same headpiece that bishops wear during religious ceremonies."

"What's a bishop?"

"A bishop is in charge of a diocese, which is a word for an area where a group of Christians live. I'm the bishop of Myra, a town that today is part of Turkey. I didn't want to become a bishop, but the Christians in Myra begged me to be their bishop and I eventually agreed."

"And your stick and that big coat—are those things a bishop uses, too?"

"Yes. The stick is my bishop's cross, and this big coat is an episcopal chasuble! A bishop's chasuble, I guess you could say!"

"I have one more question."

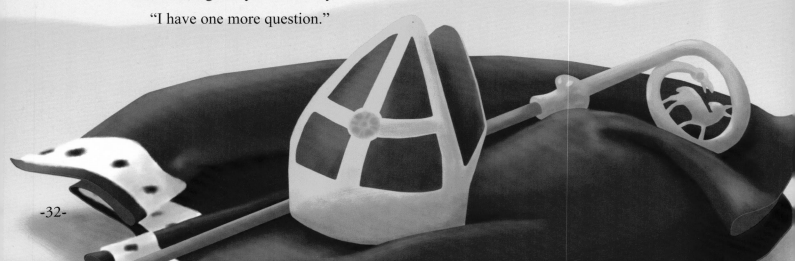

"Sure."

"Great Saint Nicolas, are you jealous of Santa Claus?"

"Santa Claus? Well, he certainly has copied me quite a bit. The red coat, the presents he gives to little children. But even though he has a white beard, compared to me, he's just a young guy! I was born in the year 270, you know, and I've been giving out gifts for centuries upon centuries. Santa Claus has only been around for a few hundred years! So don't you worry, I'm not jealous. On the contrary! The more examples of generosity we have, the better. We should all be like Saint Nicolas and give other people our time, help, and a special present or two."

"Like gingerbread!"

"Ah, I bet you'd like another piece, wouldn't you?" Saint Nicolas winks.

Emery takes the cookie Saint Nicolas hands him and thanks him before heading to the playground to pet Velvet the little donkey.

The Christmas Cacophony

All throughout the animal kingdom, the pig, the turkey, and the hedgehog could be heard singing with gusto:

"Hark, the herald angels sing . . ."

"No chance of us sleeping tonight," the jackal, the moose, and the narwhal coolly observed. "They're such terrible singers!"

Finally, the parrot, the pony, and the beetle had had enough:

"Be quiet, please! It's so awful! Have mercy on us!"

The swallow, the turtledove, and the ladybug decided they had no choice but to complain to the angels in heaven:

"It sounds like people banging on pots and pans. Do something, Gabriel. They're going to ruin Christmas!"

The angel Gabriel immediately spread his wings and flew over to talk to the pig, the turkey, and the hedgehog.

"I bring you great news. . . . Well, sort of," he said, trying to sound as brotherly as possible. "My friends, you're going to need to work on your hymns. Let's practice all together: 'do re mi . . .'"

"Silent night, holy night . . ."

But the three animals' horrendous whines eventually started to test the limits of Gabriel's angelic patience. After hours of voice coaching, the pig, the turkey, and the hedgehog were singing just as loudly and just as out of tune as before.

The elk, the grizzly, and the bat watched as Gabriel threw down his lyre in frustration.

The camel, the earthworm, and the hamster refused to give up and went to ask Saint Michael for help. After listening to their prayer, the commander of the heavenly armies went soaring through the air, determined to stop the catastrophic concert.

"Be quiet, you noisy animals—you're going to wake up our Lord!"

"Away in a manger, no crib for a bed . . ."

But the animals only hollered even louder. Saint Michael plugged his ears. "My lance can bring down dragons," he muttered, "and I know it could just as easily spear a pig, a turkey, or a hedgehog."

When they saw how angry Saint Michael was, the pig scowled, the turkey gobbled haughtily, and the hedgehog bristled. The archangel could throw his spear at them all he wanted, but no one was going to be able to stop them from singing their songs of praise.

The puma, the panda, and the koala couldn't believe their eyes. If Saint Michael had failed, who could possibly reason with this obstinate trio?

As a last resort, the annoyed animals marched all the way to the Archangel Raphael's fortress. When they arrived, the helpful angel healer was working on a bitter-tasting remedy. He knew how to turn its flavor into something as sweet as honey.

He listened to the animals' requests and said, "I'll take care of those hard-headed creatures! Tell all of the other angels that they should come, too. The more the merrier!"

"Angels we have heard on high . . ."

The pig, the turkey, and the hedgehog arrived at the manger. Baby Jesus was sleeping but the Holy Family didn't seem at all bothered by the animals' crooning.

When it came time for the chorus—"Gloria, in excelsis Deo"—a pure, beautiful sound suddenly filled the air. The animals, shepherds, and archangels were all singing in unison.

"Doesn't that sound lovely? How odd. I don't hear the three awful singers at all!" Saint Michael said from his perch on the stable roof.

"How did you manage it, dear Raphael?" Gabriel asked.

"I didn't do anything. In a choir, voices are supposed to sing all together. Some voices are deep, some voices tremble, some are high, and some people sing through their noses! But no one notices any of these imperfections when we sing as a group. If you don't want to hear the pig, the turkey, and the hedgehog, then angels and people everywhere will just have to keep singing!"

"Well then, let's sing to the glory of God, my brothers. That's what we do best!"

The Festival of Lights

*T*he city of Lyon is never as beautiful as it is on December eighth. Tonight, there are so many people in Lyon's traboules, or hidden passageways, that Noémie clings to her mother's hand. She doesn't want to miss a single moment of the Festival of Lights.

Candles are glowing in every window. Everyone in Lyon lights candles on December eighth.* The thousands of flames dancing in the night make every building look so magical!

To do her part to light up her city, Noémie had already decorated a small glass jar to hold her candle. Just before she left home, she lit the candle and placed it on the windowsill.

The little girl walks with her mother to join the torchlight procession that will leave from Saint Jean Cathedral and make its way up to Fourvière Basilica. People in the procession sing songs and say prayers to the Holy Virgin. After the ceremony, there will be a mass in the basilica led by young people from the church community.

---

* In 1852, a statue of the Virgin Mary was erected at the chapel on Fourvière Hill. The statue was inaugurated on December eighth, the Feast of the Immaculate Conception (the Immaculate Conception means that Mary was born without original sin). That night, the people of Lyon lit up their windows to thank the Virgin Mary for always protecting their city . . . from the plague, from cholera, and, soon, from war. What started as an unplanned celebration has become an important annual tradition for everyone who lives there.

After climbing the hill with the torchbearers, Noémie turns around and walks down to Place des Jacobins. The fountain in the square looks like the northern lights have fallen into it and the banks of the Saône and Rhône have been taken over by shimmering colors. Fairytale light installations are hidden just about everywhere. The town hall is crisscrossed with blue, red, and gold stripes. Statues seem to bob gently up and down, and the trees hold waterfalls of stars.

In the Parc de la Tête d'Or, there are giant carp floating on top of the grass. Shouts of amazement in every language fill the city—this four-day festival attracts tourists from all over the world!

The smell of waffles and roasted chestnuts wafts through the air. Noémie and her mother hear music and decide to follow it. This is the signal that the sound and light shows will be starting soon.

The most beautiful light displays of all are on the outside walls of Saint Jean Cathedral. Tonight, the old stones are adorned with flowers, ink, and flames. These playful images illuminate the building's sculptures and architectural wonders. How magnificent!

Standing in Place Bellecour, which has been transformed into a chest of toys, Noémie looks up at Fourvière Basilica, which was built in Mary's honor. God's mother has been watching over this city for so long. To the right of the basilica, two enormous words shine in the night.

Merci Marie

The Christmas Tree Kitten

"My list for Santa Claus is ready to send to the North Pole," Alyssa tells Papa. "Here! You can read it if you want."

Papa picks up Alyssa's letter.

Dear Santa,

For Christmas this year,
I WANT A CAT.
Chat
Katze
Gato
Gatto

You know, a cat!

I don't know what language you speak, so I thought I'd try a few different ones!
If you bring me something other than a cat again this year (like a dragon costume or a puzzle, for example), I will throw it out the window..
XOXO,
Alyssa

P.S. And don't waste your time sending me a stuffed animal like last year. I want a REAL cat.

Papa heaves a long sigh.

"Sweetie, I don't think Santa Claus has any kittens. He brings children toys, not animals!"

"And besides," Mama adds, "a cat isn't a present! It's a sensitive living creature that has to be taken care of every day!"

"But I'll take very good care of it! I'll be in charge of changing the litter and I'll take it to the vet," Alyssa promises.

Mama and Papa exchange a knowing look.

"You don't want us to have a cat, do you? Is that it? Does that mean you won't send my letter to Santa Claus?"

"Of course we will," Papa says.

"Papa and I have been thinking, Alyssa. And we've decided that since you want a cat so badly, we're going to adopt one from an animal shelter."

"Hurray!"

"But not right away," Mama says.

"Well, when?"

"After Christmas, when we have time to take a little road trip. There aren't any animal shelters near us."

"Oh," Alyssa says, very disappointed.

To try and change the subject and bring a smile back to his daughter's face, Papa makes a suggestion:

"Why don't we go pick out a Christmas tree?"

"I'd rather go pick out my cat."

"Alyssa! I said after Christmas!" Mama sounds annoyed.

"Come on, Alyssa," Papa says. "Uncle Nicolas said we could choose any tree we want. Let's get going!"

Uncle Nicolas's land is covered in tall, snow-capped trees.

Alyssa doesn't know which one to choose. They're all so beautiful. She walks over to a rather bushy spruce to get a better look when suddenly—

Meow.

"Did you hear that?" Alyssa squeals.

"What?" asks Mama.

"The tree meowed!"

"A tree that meows? Ha, ha. Very funny, Alyssa!" Papa teases.

Uncle Nicolas is getting impatient.

"So, which tree would you like?" he asks.

"I want this one," Alyssa says, pointing to the tree that meowed.

Uncle Nicolas slices through the trunk of the tree with his ax. Then Papa helps him carry it and place it carefully in the trunk of the car.

Back at the house, Papa stands up the tree in their tree holder while Mama opens the big box of Christmas decorations. She takes out all of the different colored balls, big red fabric bows, a string of lights, and a glittering star. Alyssa hangs them on the tree.

MEOW!

This time, Alyssa knows she's not imagining things. She peers through the branches and between the pine needles she sees . . . A KITTEN!

"Oh!!! He's so cute!" the little girl coos as she gently takes the little ball of fur in her arms.

Papa stares wide-eyed at the kitten that seems to have magically appeared in his daughter's lap.

Alyssa is overjoyed. "Poor baby," she murmurs to the little cat. "Lost in Uncle Nicolas's forest. You found a place to hide in the branches of our tree. How lucky is that? I'm going to call you Evergreen. My Christmas Evergreen!"

The kitten purrs happily against Alyssa's cheek.

Papa telephones Uncle Nicolas to make sure the kitten doesn't belong to anyone.

"There isn't a house for miles around," Uncle Nicolas says. "It's a miracle Alyssa chose that tree. Without her, what would have happened to that poor kitten?"

Papa tells Alyssa that it looks like Evergreen is an abandoned kitten and that yes, yes, we can keep him. Then he walks into the living room.

"Aaaaah!"

The Christmas tree has tipped over onto the carpet, all of the ornaments are broken, the kitten is tangled up in the string of lights, and Mama is running after it as fast as she can.

Alyssa is bent double with laughter, but Papa doesn't find it funny at all.

He sweeps away the pieces of broken ornaments and the pine needles all over the floor.

"This cat is nothing but trouble," he grumbles.

"Don't be mad at him!" Alyssa says. "Until today, this tree was his house! We changed all the decorations and didn't even ask his permission."

"She's right. Give him time to get used to his new home," Mama says gently.

"Fine, but there will have to be a few rules!" Papa says sternly.

Papa builds a fence around the Christmas tree, but the next day he finds the tree lying on the floor again. Evergreen is scratching the trunk with his claws. He made it through the fence without any trouble at all!

"My cute little cat is so clever!" Alyssa says, squeezing him against her.

But Papa hasn't given up yet. The next day, he decides to wrap the tree in cellophane. The kitten's claws won't be able to get to it now.

This time, Mama disagrees with his plan.

"That's our Christmas tree? It looks like a giant green sausage!"

Alyssa giggles.

Ever since Evergreen came to live with them, everything has been so much more fun!

"Well, what should we do?" Papa says as he unwraps the tree.

"Christmas is tomorrow! We have to have some kind of Christmas tree." Mama looks worried.

"I have an idea!" Alyssa cries. "Why don't we attach the Christmas tree to the ceiling?"

King's Cake

Melchior has had enough. The magi king has blisters on his feet, his right leg is hurting, and his back muscles have turned to jelly. The gold he's carrying in his bag has never seemed so heavy, so useless, and so inconvenient. To make matters worse, he is now lost in a foreign country: a veil of mist has suddenly fallen over his path and he can no longer see the caravan that was following him or even the animal he's riding. He is helpless and alone in the fog. Melchior scratches his long white beard and squints to try and see beyond the tip of his nose. Nothing. He can't see a thing. The world around him is gray. What sadness he feels! The star he left everything for has disappeared right when he needed it the most. He begins to doubt himself. What is he doing here?

Why did he ever leave in the first place? He's too old to be running after stars, isn't he?

He stops for a moment to calm down and pray. When he opens his eyes, he sees a luminous point of light dancing in the distance. Could it be his beloved star? He hurries toward it . . . but it's only a roaring fire. A man with dark skin is cooking some kind of flat pastry. Melchior greets him joyfully, introduces himself, and asks why on earth the man has decided to camp here.

"No particular reason," the strange man chuckles. "I thought that instead of wandering around in the fog like a lost soul, I'd make myself something to eat! I can rest and regain my strength while I wait for the star to reappear."

Melchior jumps when he hears the man, whose name is Balthazar, mention the star. The other sages had treated him with such scorn and the caravan travelers had been so uninterested in what he was saying that the magi king had assumed he was the only one who could see the star. But Balthazar is looking for it, too! Melchior can tell from the man's colorful clothes, worn sandals, and enormous camel that he has traveled from far away, just like him. Melchior quickly learns that this bizarre cook is also a well-known astronomer in his home country.

While the two men are passionately discussing the constellations above them, a third man appears. He, too, was drawn by the fire . . . and he, too, is lost.

"My brothers," says Balthazar, "let's sit down together and enjoy this cake."

Without thinking twice, the other two men sit down next to the fire. The third traveler's name is Gaspar. He is very young and comes from the Far East. His skin is copper-colored and his beautiful clothes smell pleasantly of incense. He rubs his neck and sighs.

"My neck is killing me . . . it must be all that time I spent watching that star."

Melchior can't believe his luck. In the middle of nowhere, he has stumbled upon two other star-seekers!

Gaspar heats water for tea while Balthazar removes his round, golden cake from the fire. He divides it into three pieces and hands one to each of the other men.

"This is a specialty in my country," Balthazar explains. "The cake is filled with almond cream."

"This is delicious!" Gaspar exclaims as he throws dried leaves into the boiling water.

"Divine!" Melchior adds, savoring every bite.

"Just make sure you don't break a tooth. One of the buttons on my coat fell into the batter and I couldn't find it to fish it out!"

A few minutes later, Melchior finds the shiny button in his piece of cake. The venerable magi king brandishes it as if it were buried treasure and the two other men applaud to congratulate him.

After eating the cake and drinking Gaspar's delicious tea, Melchior feels reinvigorated. Then Balthazar makes an announcement.

"The fog has lifted," he says. "I think Melchior should lead the way from now on. He is the most experienced among us and he found my lost button . . . he'll know how to take us wherever the star wants us to go!"

The old magi king nods. Suddenly, his leg doesn't hurt as badly as before. His burden is lighter because now it is shared.

On his journey, he has found brothers filled with the same hope he feels. He knows that all the gold he is carrying is worth far less than the friendships forged on these dusty footpaths.

With the star shining brightly above him, Melchior stands up. Gaspar and Balthazar do the same. The mysterious celestial body has suddenly reappeared in the sky, inviting the men to start walking again. Together.

December 11
Italy
The Greccio Nativity

On the steep path that leads to Greccio, a man in a homespun robe was throwing pieces of bread to the birds. The walker wore a cheerful smile and had eyes that seemed to shine with all of the beauty of the mountains around him. His name was Francis. While he fed the birds, he talked to them about how happy he was that he would soon reach the tiny Italian village peeking through the trees. He had come here to celebrate Christmas with his fellow monks.

When he reached the village perched on top of the hill, the villagers welcomed him warmly. Francis was planning an exceptional Christmas Eve celebration for them, including a living nativity scene with live animals in a grotto in Greccio. The villagers wouldn't have seen anything like this before, but Saint Francis wanted to make the mystery of the Incarnation real to them: God became a baby! He wanted everyone to understand who Jesus really was and why he called himself the "child of Bethlehem."

That night, December 24, 1223, people came from all over the valley carrying lanterns and torches to climb the mountain for midnight mass. They were drawn by the singing of the monks echoing through the forest and by the rumor that a great saint had come to spend Christmas in Greccio. As they entered the grotto, they saw an ox and donkey, sprays of herbs and colorful flowers, and in the manger was a beautiful sleeping baby, the living image of Jesus Christ.

The manger filled with straw also served as the priest's pulpit. The child in it was sleeping soundly. Francis picked up the baby ever so gently and the little one opened his eyes, grabbed the monk's beard, and laughed. In that moment, the believers gathered together in the grotto realized that even if the Jesus in their hearts seemed to have fallen asleep, Francis's words and example had woken Him up.

Under the bright, beautiful stars, Francis preached a sermon about joy. That service was never forgotten. The people of Greccio talked so much about the marvels of that holy night that the following year, they re-created the scene of Jesus's birth again in grottos and stables around the village.

And that is how Saint Francis of Assisi reinvented the way people experience Christmas. Ever since then, all over the world, in homes and in churches, believers young and old display a manger scene to celebrate the Nativity.

Lupita's Bouquet

On December twelfth, Mexicans celebrate the Feast of Our Lady of Guadalupe, the patron saint of Mexico. This is a very important day for Christians in the Americas.

Like many other pilgrims, a little Indian girl named Lupita has decided to go to the shrine of Our Lady of Guadalupe to pay homage to the Virgin who appeared on the hill in Tepeyac.*

Lupita would like to place a gift for the Virgin and her child under the tilma. After all, soon it will be Jesus's birthday! There are thirteen days left before Christmas. Mary is about to give birth. In Mexico, everyone knows that Our Lady of Guadalupe is pregnant. The double belt she wears over her belly is a sign.

The problem is, Lupita has nothing to give them.

In the hut she lives in with her grandfather, there are no Christmas decorations and not a single peso to spend on the smallest gift.

"Don't cry, Lupita, indita mía," her grandfather says. "You're so clever, I'm sure you'll find something to give Our Lady."

Lupita dries her tears and hugs her grandfather. She thinks about the Virgin of Guadalupe's pink dress and remembers that it is decorated with mountain flowers. That's what she'll do! Lupita will pick wildflowers on the way to the church in Tepeyac and give them to Mary.

---

* In 1531, in northern Mexico, the mother of God revealed herself to an Aztec man named Juan Diego. On December 12, 1531, an image of Mary miraculously appeared on his tilma, or cape. This tilma is still on display in the church that was built to honor Our Lady.

The little girl confidently heads for the hills. But after foraging for flowers just about everywhere, she can't find even the tiniest daisy.

Lupita gives up and gathers some plain green leaves instead.

When she enters the church, the pilgrims carrying fancy gifts make fun of her:

"Look at this poor little Indian with her weeds . . ."

"A bouquet of leaves, what a silly idea!"

"What kind of present for Our Lady is that?"

But Lupita doesn't listen to them. She keeps walking to the front of the church. The little girl places her offering beneath the tilma and suddenly, before the dumbfounded eyes of everyone in the church, the green leaves turn bright red. The little Indian girl has given the Virgin a bouquet of scarlet stars. How beautiful!

Everyone wants to get a closer look at the miracle. The unkind tongues immediately repent and offer Lupita gifts.

And so the little girl leaves the church with her arms full of presents! On Christmas Day, she already knows she'll be back with another bouquet for the Virgin.

The Mexican people will not forget the marvelous plant* that blooms in crimson stars. Today it is still called flor de nochebuena, or "flower of the Holy Night."

* The red-leafed "flower of the Holy Night" is also known as the poinsettia. In 1825, Joel Poinsett, the first United States ambassador to Mexico, returned to his home country with cuttings from the plant, and the spectacular red flower was named the poinsettia in his honor. Today it adorns homes and churches around the world during Advent. The church in Tepeyac, which became the Basilica of Our Lady of Guadalupe in 1904, is known for its particularly abundant poinsettia displays.

$\mathcal{S}$aint Lucia

$\mathcal{S}$vea has woken up very early this morning. After getting out of bed, she brushes her blond hair then puts on a white gown and a red sash. When that's all done, she places a crown of candles on her head.

Today is Saint Lucia Day. Today, she is Saint Lucia.

Her heart beating fast with excitement, she goes downstairs to the kitchen. Her little brothers Gunnar and Kai are already up and dressed as star boys, hopping around the table wearing pointed hats decorated with stars and holding star wands.

The three children make breakfast together. They place cups of coffee and delicious saffron buns called lussekatt on a large tray.

On their tiptoes, the children climb the stairs.

In front of the door to their parents' bedroom, Gunnar and Kai light Svea's crown of candles. This crown is the symbol of Lucia's story. People say that she brought food to the poor people in her village every night, and since her arms were always filled with presents for them, she eventually decided to put candles on her head to light her way in the dark.

This morning, Svea is the one carrying wonderful things to eat.

The children enter the bedroom without a sound. Then Svea sings the Saint Lucia song.

Their parents wake up. They are thrilled to see their children standing around them on Saint Lucia Day. Their daughter has such a pretty voice, and she knows all of the traditional songs. Svea's mother and father are so proud that this year Svea was chosen by her classmates to be Saint Lucia. Later today, she will walk through the streets at the head of a procession of other young girls in white dresses. Her friends will carry candles in their hands while Svea, her hands clasped in front of her, will proudly wear her sparkling crown.

To end the day, Svea will attend the Saint Lucia concert at the church in the village. But shhh . . . the sun is coming up and Svea, eyes shining, is already singing:

Night walks grand, yet silent,
Now hear its gentle wings,
In every room so hushed,
Whispering like wings.
Look, at our threshold stands,
White-clad with light in her hair,
Santa Lucia, Santa Lucia!

Darkness shall take flight soon,
From earth's valleys.
So she speaks a
Wonderful word to us:
A new day will rise again
From the rosy sky . . .
Santa Lucia, Santa Lucia!

The House of Bread

Today, my older brother Tiago and my older sister Catarina took the nativity figurines out of their box. It was time to set up our nativity scene! These little ceramic people are very fragile so we handled each one carefully. Unfortunately, we were so concentrated on what we were doing that we weren't paying attention to our little brother João. The little rascal walked right onto the stable and crushed it under his feet!

What a disaster! Now the Holy Family had nowhere to live! All of us were terribly worried because we knew that Saint Joseph hadn't been able to find a place for the Virgin at the inn. And we had just managed to break the one place they had finally found to take shelter. . . .

"We'll just have to move them into my princess castle," Catarina said. "It's perfect! Jesus is the son of God; he deserves to be born in a palace."

Tiago refused. "No! We can't put the Holy Family in a flashy palace. God was born a poor baby in a poor family. He chose to make Himself small and lowly to show us how much He loves us. So a princess castle doesn't make any sense at all!"

"I've got a box," I said. "If we put some crumpled tissue paper inside, it could make a perfect grotto!"

"But that's what everyone does!" Tiago shook his head.

"Why don't we just re-create the whole village of Bethlehem?" Catarina suggested.

"We don't have time for that!" Tiago replied in frustration. "Your idea is too complicated!"

"Everything is always too complicated for you!" Catarina scowled.

I could tell they were about to get into a huge fight. And all because of a nativity scene. It was so silly!

Luckily, the blessed hour of snack time arrived just in time. Papa brought in chocolate and an enormous broa fresh out of the oven and that got everyone to calm down. Broa is a Portuguese specialty. It's a kind of corn bread with a thick, crunchy crust that Papa makes better than anybody.

He set it on the table and said, "Children, did you know that Bethlehem means 'house of bread' in Hebrew? 'Bet Lehem'?"

"What a strange name for a place!" I said.

Papa cut a slice from the round loaf and explained.

"It's not so strange if you think about it! Jesus is the bread of life, sent down from heaven. When we take communion at church, He is offering Himself as nourishment. That's the mystery of the eucharist!"

"Now I understand why God chose to be born in Bethlehem!" Tiago exclaimed. "And why Mary lay Jesus in a manger."

My big brother is so smart, I thought to myself as I sneaked another piece of bread.

"Hey, what are you doing to our snack?" Catarina yelled.

My big sister was not happy that I'd been pulling out and eating pieces from the middle of the loaf but I don't like the crust, and Papa had baked the broa a little too long so the one on this loaf was even harder than usual! I didn't want her to be angry at me, so I had to think of something.

"I'm making . . . Jesus's house!"

Turns out this was a good idea! Papa carved out the rest of the loaf so that only the crust was left, then we all shared the bread and placed the figurines inside their golden-brown grotto. The Holy Family looked happy in their new home. Our nativity scene was beautiful and original . . . and looked good enough to eat!

The Knight with the Frozen Heart

Many years ago in England there lived a knight named Owen. Wherever he went, this armored giant told people that he was fearless, blameless, and godless. Just as they did every year, his eleven brothers in arms begged him to accompany them to a Christmas Eve church service. But as usual, Owen left his friends at the church door.

"Christmas is founded on a ridiculous story!" he scoffed. "A god who transforms himself into a baby? How can you believe that? Why would the creator of all things become human? I'd rather stay with the horses than sing those stupid hymns with you!"

His companions went into the church and Owen stomped off to the stables. He unbridled the twelve horses, removed their saddles, groomed them, and gave them water and plenty of hay. But when these tasks were done, the knight still didn't feel any calmer than before. He walked in circles in the stable like a lion in a cage. Then he put a saddle and bridle on his own horse and decided to go out for a ride. Maybe the forest snow would cool his anger. He was still so filled with rage about Christmas that he slammed the door behind him and forgot to fasten the latch to lock it.

Owen trotted on his glowing horse between the white pines until he reached the edge of a small frozen lake in the shape of a heart. In the middle of the frozen water was a tree with golden branches, each one heavy with delicious-looking red apples. His horse loved treats and wanted to walk out onto the ice to eat the miraculous fruit, but Owen held him back. The knight was afraid that the ice would crack under their weight. He got down from his horse and threw a stone at the tree. It disappeared instantly into the water. Just as he had feared, the layer of ice was far too thin to walk on.

So Owen contemplated this strange landscape in silence and regretted that he couldn't get closer to the breathtaking tree to uncover whatever mystery had placed it here. The place was so beautiful that Owen's anger vanished into thin air.

Suddenly, on the other side of the lake, he saw the shadows of several horses galloping. He counted eleven and went pale. He recognized these horses—they belonged to his fellow knights! No, no! How could this be? In that instant, Owen remembered that he hadn't latched the stable door. The animals had only had to push it open to escape into the snowy forest.

The horses stared at the golden tree and seemed irresistibly drawn to the fruit hanging from its branches. Owen knew that, like his horse, they would try to walk onto the frozen lake and would perish in its freezing depths. How could he prevent them from walking onto the ice? The burly knight decided to try banging his sword against his shield. It made such a commotion that the large animals stepped back, but as soon as he stopped, the horses returned to the deadly waters as if bewitched by the tree. Owen chased them around the lake, trying to lead them back to the stables, but at every turn, the fugitives managed to slip from between his fingers.

After an hour of galloping in vain through the snow, Owen started shouting.

"These cursed nags don't understand anything! I want to save them and all I'm doing is terrorizing them with my coat of armor and my sword! They're all going to die, and I can't do anything about it. What a horrible Christmas present for my dear friends!"

Owen threw his shield and sword into the snow and kept chasing the horses, but he still couldn't catch them. Exhausted by the absurd battle and unable to make the animals understand the danger they were facing, he got off his horse.

He held his face in his freezing fingers and moaned, "I am as stupid as these stupid horses! If only I were a horse, then I could rescue my friends' steeds and repair the wrong I have done!"

No sooner had he said these words than the tree in the middle of the lake burst into flames. The horses stopped their frenzied racing to watch as the trunk and branches were consumed by the fire. This burning bush would soon melt the ice. Owen suddenly felt warmth spreading throughout his entire body. White hairs sprouted on his skin, his nose grew long into a horse's muzzle, and his own hair transformed into a silver mane. Where the ice had been there was now pure, shimmering water. And where the knight in armor had been standing, a white stallion was pawing the ground. Owen was a horse! He marched through the snow in his brand-new hooves and his trusted horse followed close behind.

Now that he was one of them, Owen was easily able to approach the eleven lost horses. They recognized him as one of their own and followed him obediently to the stable. Once he was sure the herd was safe and warm, Owen walked outside and latched the door with the tip of his muzzle.

The bell rang for midnight mass, and Owen the stallion stood at the church door and wept. He had to become a horse in order to save his friends' horses, just as God had to become a man to save mankind. This is why He had taken the form of a baby in a manger, this is why He had lived among men. The knight had been transformed into an animal and was finally able to admit what he now knew was true: humans, like animals, will only follow someone who they know understands them and resembles them.

The snow melted under Owen's warm tears, and in the midst of his weeping, his new faith was born. The horsehair on his legs disappeared, his body reared back onto two legs, and his limbs returned to their normal length. He saw his hands, his face, and his human body once again. The only thing that remained changed by this adventure was his burning heart.

Owen turned and walked into the church. His eleven companions welcomed him with joy.

Mistralou and the Thirteen Desserts

Leona lays three tablecloths on the Christmas dinner table and then arranges the desserts. One, two, three, four . . . thirteen plates in all. Perfect!

Her guests are going to love them. These thirteen desserts will be the perfect ending to what people in Provence call the Great Supper. Next, Leona sets three candles on the table. In the fireplace, a large log is slowly burning. The young woman sprays it with wine and recites the traditional prayer:

"May God give us the grace to live until next year. And if there are not more of us, may there not be any fewer!"

In a darkened corner of the room, a mischievous elf is listening to her and rubbing his belly. The pointed cap on his head and the sprig of thyme tucked behind his ear leave no room for doubt: this is Mistralou, the elf of Provence. He is as greedy as a pig and as troublesome as the wind.

After frolicking around in the woods and shrubs all night, the mouth-watering smells emanating from the beautiful Leona's house proved so tempting that he decided to slip inside.

Mistralou waits for the cook to leave the room and then jumps onto the table, staining the white tablecloth with his dirty feet.

"Thirteen desserts, and all for me!" he squeals in his lilting voice.

He begins by turning around the four bowls of mendiants. Mendiants are dried fruit and nuts that represent the four mendicant (or begging) orders of the Church. They certainly look tasty!

First dessert: a dried fig whose grayish, wrinkly coating is supposed to resemble a Franciscan monk's habit. Mistralou devours it with great respect.

Second dessert: a crunchy almond that happens to be the same pale brown color as the tunics worn by Dominican monks.

"Mm, delicious," the elf murmurs from his perch on the edge of the table.

Now he's reached the hazelnuts and decides to juggle a few before stuffing them in his mouth. Yum! Third dessert! The color of the hazelnuts vaguely reminds him of the Carmelites' brown robes, but the round nuts mostly make him think of the trails covered in autumn leaves he was running around on not so long ago.

Finally, the fourth dessert and the last of the mendiants: raisins to remember the Augustinian brothers! He gobbles them up by the handful.

"Those mendiants really worked up my appetite! Where's my fifth dessert?" the ravenous elf wonders.

On the next plate is a sweet flatbread called pompe à l'huile. Mistralou bites off a hefty chunk and comments between bites.

"This, mmm, flavor . . . the olive oil . . . mmm, the orange blossom . . . is, mmm, utterly delightful!"

Sixth dessert. Mistralou pours himself a glass of mulled wine and dips his piece of bread in it.

"Simmered over a woodfire in the old provençale tradition . . . this wine is divine."

Glass in hand, the little glutton throws himself onto the seventh dish, which contains a gigantic block of quince paste. Mistralou licks his fingers. The paste is perfectly sticky and sprinkled with little grains of sugar.

Eighth dessert: Mistralou wolfs down a bar of white Montélimar nougat.

"What a tasty blend of almonds, sugar, and honey!" he says with a hop. His skipping eventually leads him to the ninth dessert: a Swiss chard tart from Nice. This cake is coated in icing sugar and stuffed with Swiss chard, pine nuts, and raisins. It melts in the little elf's mouth.

"This is the most astonishing provençal dessert of all," the gourmet-loving elf says in ecstasy. "And the sweetest green cake ever!"

Tenth dessert: all eyes on the calissons from Aix! These treats made with candied melon and almond are so scrumptious that the elf can't help but spin around.

Eleventh dessert: it's time for the little gentleman to gorge himself on candied fruit from Apt. He finds angelica stems, cherries, pears, and citron. And he tries them all!

Twelfth dessert: Mistralou clicks his heels together beside a dish of dried fruit stuffed with almond paste. He picks up a stuffed date and takes just one bite before declaring, "How absolutely succulent!"

By now, the little glutton is starting to feel a little heavy. . . .

"But I want my last dessert," he mumbles to himself as he staggers across the table.

Mistralou drags himself over to the basket of fresh fruit. To digest his twelve previous desserts, he chooses a fragrant orange, which he peels conscientiously before devouring its juicy segments. Years ago, an orange was often the only gift children received for Christmas. Today, it's a bonus dessert.

"And a wonderful one at that!" he sings.

Suddenly, the door opens and Leona appears.

"For crying out loud!" she yells. "My beautiful table is ruined! Get out of here, you pesky elf!"

In reply, Mistralou lets out a loud burp.

Furious, Leona swings her broom in the little good-for-nothing's direction.

But Mistralou is already gone, faster than the wind and just as impossible to catch.

The Bird Tree

Not far from the manger stands an immense olive tree. In its branches, the birds of the sky have perched to get a better view of the most beautiful child the universe has ever seen. They blend their songs with the singing of the angels to celebrate his birth.

What an unusual Christmas tree! Doves, hummingbirds, and so many others appear to have been swept up into what looks like a ball of lively foliage.

The shepherds look up at the longest branch and count hundreds of different colored wings.

Suddenly, a baby sparrow appears beneath the glittering Star. Light as a feather, like a snowflake, the fledgling lands delicately on the tip of the branch. There is only a little bit of room for his tiny feet. Then . . .

Crack! The beautiful branch breaks . . . and all the birds fly away.

The sleeping child opens his eyes to the sky and watches as a swarm of feathers rises up to the moon.

For hours, those doves and hummingbirds had sat squeezed together, balancing on the olive tree's branches. And then, because of a little sparrow that weighed almost nothing, everything was turned upside down. Now the birds have dispersed to the four corners of the world to sing to the glory of God.

As if the weight of a miniscule bird could change everything. As if the presence of a tiny little baby were enough to spread love everywhere.

*P*aper Cranes

*S*husaku silently picks up a square piece of paper. A pretty blue-patterned sheet that he folds into a triangle. He folds down the corners, flattens the edges, and turns over the folds he has made. He does all of this without thinking. After a few minutes, a turquoise crane appears between his expert fingers.

Since the beginning of the Advent season, Shusaku has made fifty cranes in all different colors.

As a Christian in Japan, this is how he gets ready for Christmas.

Making an origami crane is a way to say a prayer for peace.

Making an origami crane is a way to honor the memory of Sadako Sasaki.

Shusaku thinks about the little girl from Hiroshima as he tugs on his cranes' wings.

Like all Japanese children, he learned about Sadako's story at school.

It begins in 1945 with the dropping of the atomic bomb over Hiroshima.

The city was destroyed in an instant and thousands of Japanese people were killed.

Sadako, who was only two years old, miraculously survived the bombing even though she was less than two miles away from the explosion.

She grew up and became a joyful, athletic young girl and a good student. But when she was eleven, Sadako became seriously ill because of radiation from the atomic bomb.

To cheer her up, Sadako's best friend told her about the legend of the thousand cranes. "Anyone who folds one thousand paper cranes will have their wish granted."

All they had to do to cure her leukemia was fold one thousand paper cranes. Their wings would carry Sadako's prayer.

So Sadako started folding cranes. Every piece of paper that passed through her hands, no matter how small, was transformed into a magnificent bird. She even used the labels on her medicine bottles.

After folding her 644th crane, Sadako died despite all of her faith and courage. She was twelve years old.

Her classmates and friends finished folding the thousand cranes.

Many years after Sadako's death, children in Japan and around the world still make origami cranes and send them to Hiroshima in memory of the children who were killed by the bomb and the war.

Thanks to Sadako, the crane has become an international symbol for peace.

On Christmas Eve, Shusaku will send his birds to Hiroshima.

There is a statue there of a little girl holding a golden crane and wearing origami necklaces that twirl in the wind. The children's monument bears the following inscription:

This is our cry,
This is our prayer:
To build peace in the world.

In Joseph's Arms

My beloved—your mother—
has carried you for nine months.

But I haven't felt you against me until now,
my child.

Can you hear the beating of my heart?
When I witnessed the mystery of your birth,
I forgot all about the doors that were closed
in our faces and all of our wandering.

Yes, you are here!
And nothing can tarnish my joy.
My treasure, my miracle, my baby,
Sleep now, in the fortress of my arms.

I will serve you and your mother,
I will love you both more than my own life.

And if we must leave and travel far,
I will guide you both down every path.
Wherever we go, I will build houses.
You will not sleep in this manger for long.
I will carve a cradle out of wood for my
little king.

I can already hear your first word:
"Abba . . . Father!"
And even if I know you're talking to the
heavens,
I'll come running and say, "Here I am."

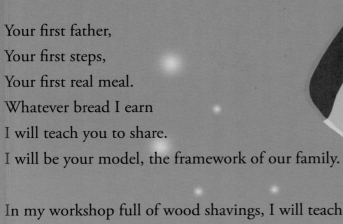

Your first father,
Your first steps,
Your first real meal.
Whatever bread I earn
I will teach you to share.
I will be your model, the framework of our family.

In my workshop full of wood shavings, I will teach
you to work with wood, to read the Scriptures,
and to stand up for everything that is good and
beautiful.
Or are you the one who will be teaching me?

You are smiling at the angels. There are thousands
all around.
I say nothing but I believe the strange dreams they
whispered to me in the night.

My baby, so great and so small.
Today I receive you.
My Jesus, I love you. I adore you.

Trinity's List

Lindsay is running all over the place and making piles of lists to make sure she doesn't forget anything. The party she's organizing for Christmas has to be perfect!

Trinity is playing cards by herself. With all her planning, Mom doesn't really have time to do anything fun with her.

"Sweetheart, don't forget to give me a list of the presents you want for Christmas!" Lindsay reminds her daughter while she bustles around the kitchen.

"Another list?!" Trinity groans and drops her cards on the table.

But Lindsay doesn't hear her daughter. The young mother is too busy writing down everything she has to do to get ready.

Trinity reads the to-do list her mother has hung on the refrigerator door. She looks puzzled.

"Mom, I think you forgot the most important thing!"

"Really? What did I forget? You can add it to the list if you want to, sweetheart!"

So Trinity takes a pencil and rewrites her mom's list:

TO DO LIST

* Invite the family and our elderly neighbor
* ~~Buy presents~~ Be present
* ~~Wrap presents~~ Marvel at the gift God has given us
* ~~Set up~~ Pray around the nativity scene
* Send ~~Christmas cards~~ love
* Prepare ~~Christmas decorations~~ our hearts for the coming of Jesus
* Choose ~~party outfit~~ to clothe ourselves with joy
* Light up ~~the Christmas tree~~ the world
* ~~Listen to~~ Live the pastor's Christmas message

When she reads her daughter's words, a smile lights up Lindsay's face.
At last she turns to Trinity and takes her in her arms.

Babushka's Soup

The wind and snow are whipping fiercely against the steppe. Aly looks at the frozen landscape from behind the isba, or log cabin, window. Next to the fire licking the bottom of the soup pot, the little boy is nice and warm. He inhales the wonderful aroma spreading around the room. Babushka stirs the borscht she has just made. Borscht is a winter soup made with beets and potatoes. Because times are hard in the village, there is not very much in the pot. Just enough to fill two bowls.

No matter, it's more than enough for both of us, the little boy thinks to himself as he adds a little water to the pot to make it last longer.

Babushka and Aly are about to eat when someone knocks on the door of the isba. His grandmother opens it to find old Pavel has come to wish them a merry Christmas and sing them a song. He's as thin as a rail, but he sings happily and accompanies himself on his balalaika.

When he has finished his song, Aly claps and Babushka says,

"Sit down, Pavel. Would you like to share a bowl of borscht?"

"I wouldn't say no, Babushka," the old musician replies.

"Aly," the distinguished old lady whispers in her grandson's ear, "please add a bowl of water to our soup for Pavel."

"Yes, Babu."

Aly would have liked to add meat and beets to the pot instead . . . but there's nothing left. So he dilutes the borscht like Babushka asked him to and heats the pot again.

The little boy takes another look out the window and sees three children sitting on the side of the road. They look like the widow Anja's children. Outside in the freezing cold? How can that be? But Babushka has already opened her door.

"Come in, children, our isba is warm and a bowl of steaming broth will do you good!"

The grandmother sits the three children down around the table just as Pavel strikes up a new song.

Aly knows exactly what he's supposed to do and adds three bowls of water to the pot before stoking the fire. When the soup is finally hot and everyone is rubbing their hands together at the thought of dinner, they hear three knocks on the door. Who could it be now?

This time it's a traveling stranger looking for a place to stay.

"Here," the man says, "I can give you some borodinsky in exchange for a little warmth." He hands Babushka a large loaf of brown bread with coriander seeds.

"Welcome, traveler. We don't have much, but we are happy to share it with you nonetheless," Babushka replies.

The man shakes the snow from his coat and sits down at the table between Pavel and Anja's oldest child. He tears the borodinsky bread into six pieces. *At least the children will be able to crumble it into their soup to make it a little thicker,* Aly thinks as he adds another bowl of water to the pot.

Now the pot is half full. A few minutes ago, there was just a little bit of soup at the bottom. The little boy has never seen a broth so clear. The soup is almost transparent, with only a few pieces of potato floating here and there. The borscht has been diluted five times. Aly's stomach growls in despair.

Babushka sees the disappointment on his face.

"What is the opposite of poverty?" she asks in a whisper.

"Being rich," Aly replies almost immediately.

Babushka shakes her head.

"Not at all. The opposite of being poor is sharing."

His grandmother carries the pot to the table. The stranger stands and thanks his hosts for their hospitality and for the meal they are about to share. Pavel nods in agreement and the three children offer a smile. Aly sits down.

Babushka lifts the lid and plunges her ladle into the soup. The guests' faces light up. A marvelous smell begins to fill the isba.

Aly can't believe his nostrils and leans over the pot. It is filled almost to the brim with a thick, succulent liquid.

When everyone has been served, Aly lifts the first spoonful to his lips.

He closes his eyes and savors the best borscht he has ever eaten.

December 22
Mayotte
Laëtitia and Laylati

A bit of earth lost in the Indian Ocean.
A little piece of France between East Africa and Madagascar.
A turquoise lagoon where the green turtles and kwassa-kwassa* glide.
This is Mayotte, the island of one thousand perfumes.

There are no snow-covered pine trees here in the month of December, but the jacaranda and flamboyant trees are in full bloom. The whole island sizzles with color, and to Laëtitia, it's even prettier than the Christmas lights on the grand boulevards back in Paris. Here in Mayotte, it looks like thousands of mauve butterflies have landed in the jacaranda branches and the red flamboyants seem to burn with flames of joy.

December is also fruit season! Laëtitia shares delicious mangoes and juicy lychees with her best friend, Laylati. Laylati always wears long dresses with pretty printed patterns on them and puts jasmine flowers in her braided hair. She lives in a traditional Mahoran house called a banga in the village of Bouéni. Across the street from her banga is Laëtitia's house.

People in Mayotte don't celebrate Christmas. Like most Mahorans, Laylati is Muslim and hasn't heard very much about Jesus. So Laëtitia talks to her about Him. She tells her that on Christmas, the day Jesus was born, children who have been good are given gifts. When she lived in Paris, on Christmas Eve Laëtitia would hang stockings underneath the chimney and the next day they would be filled with surprises.

-84-

* Comorian fishing boats. These boats are often used by Comorian migrants to reach the beaches of Mayotte.

"Don't worry, Laylati," Laëtitia says to her friend, "you'll have gifts on Christmas, too. You're so nice and you work so hard in school. I'm sure Santa Claus will remember you! Just leave your boots or flip flops outside your house."

Laëtitia also invites Laylati to have dinner with her family on Christmas Day.

"We're going to have a voulé* on Robinson Beach. Papa's going to grill fish, breadfruit, and a whole duck on the barbecue. Mama is going to make vanilla sauce to serve with everything, and for dessert, my brother is making a pineapple tart. We'll swim all day, drink mango juice, and play in the sand with our toys. It's going to be great!"

Laylati smiles. "Oustawi! Nitsoja!" she says in Shimaore,** which means, "Awesome! I'll be there!"

Now Laylati is just as excited for Christmas as Laëtitia is. Together the two friends make a Christmas tree out of banana leaves and decorate it with shells they find on the beach.

Soon Christmas Eve arrives and it's time for Laëtitia to put on her angel costume.

She places her neon pink rubber boots just outside her front door. On the other side of the street, Laylati waves to get her attention. Just like her friend, she's putting her shoes next to the door. She hopes she'll get the presents Laëtitia told her about!

"Why are you wearing that pretty costume?" she asks Laëtitia.

"I'm playing an angel in the living nativity tonight! My papa sewed it for me," Laëtitia says proudly. "I'll let you borrow it."

* Traditional Mahoran beach barbecue.
** Language spoken in Mayotte.

The little girl runs to hug her friend before getting in the car with her parents.

Tonight, Laëtitia's whole family is going to Mamoudzou (Mayotte's capital) for a Christmas Eve service. Notre Dame de Fatima is the only church on Grande-Terre, the main island of Mayotte, and tonight it's bursting at the seams!

Laëtitia makes sure her angel costume looks just right and joins the twenty other children onstage to recreate the birth of Christ. Some of the children are Mahoran and others are Malagasy and Comorian. The living nativity scene at Notre Dame de Fatima is anything but dull, and laughter echoes throughout the church—especially when a three-year-old shepherd runs off with the Baby Jesus doll! Mary looks horrified, but luckily Joseph restores order in the stable fairly quickly and the angels sing a gospel song. The audience claps and cheers and the priest enters with the children's choir. The Christmas service begins in a spirit of reverence and joy.

When she gets home from Mamoudzou, Laëtitia rushes over to her neon pink boots. They're overflowing with presents: coconut wood jewelry, little bottles of ylang-ylang perfume, rag dolls wearing tiny salouvas,* and plenty of candies. How lovely! Santa Claus has been so generous this year!

Laëtitia wonders if Laylati knows that Santa Claus has delivered his presents. The lights are off at her Mahoran neighbors' house.

* Traditional Mahoran dress.

Laëtitia crosses the street and peeks through Laylati's bedroom window. She sees her friend sleeping peacefully. Her boots are still lined up on the doormat . . . but . . . they're empty!

Suddenly Laëtitia feels very sad.

How could Santa Claus be such a scatterbrain? He forgot about Laylati!

This is so unfair. Her friend deserves to be spoiled, too.

Maybe Santa Claus couldn't see Laylati's boots in the dark because they're black, not neon pink like Laëtitia's. But still, he should have been paying more attention!

Without hesitating, Laëtitia gets one of her neon pink boots and empties the treasures it contains into her friend's boots.

On the other side of the street, her mother calls her in a worried voice:

"Laëtitia, where are you?"

"Over here, Mama!"

"Come and go to bed right now or you'll be too tired to enjoy the voulé."

Laëtitia walks back to her mother and slips into bed without even taking off her white angel wings. She falls asleep instantly.

In her dreams, she can already picture Laylati's smile when she sees her gifts tomorrow morning.

The Smell of Christmas

I haven't been able to see or hear anything for ages. Since my sense of smell is all I have left, I drag my snout around just about everywhere to sniff out whatever I can! My world is colored by smells, and that's just fine for an old shepherd's dog like me.

On that unforgettable night, I was walking beside my master. He smelled just like his sheep: a familiar bouquet of musk, wool, and dried grass.

For some reason, there were a lot of us on the roads that night, and a thousand smells floated over the ground. The smells of a crowd of people walking, the familiar aroma of the flocks, and the scent of flowers inexplicably in bloom . . .

The stars that were surely shining over Bethlehem poured out a delicious perfume over the countryside. As we got closer to our destination, this indescribable fragrance grew stronger and stronger.

At last, we arrived in front of the stable. Yes, it was definitely a stable. I detected the odors of fresh straw, a fire crackling outside, animal dung, the warm breath of an ox, and soft donkey hair.

But then, all of a sudden, I wasn't so sure where I was. A stable? Really? Now that I was inside, I recognized the exquisite smell of myrrh. This had to be a temple. Woody, bitter-smelling incense smoke rose from the corners of the room like prayers going up to heaven. Now I was really doubting myself. Had my nose somehow decided to trick me?

To add to my confusion, I felt fingers heavy with rings gently place themselves on my head. The hand petting me smelled like exotic and expensive perfume. The man had two companions with him. One man's beard gave off a fruity, spicy fragrance, and on the clothes of the other man, I could distinguish aromas that I was sure came from the Far East. There was something magical . . . starlike . . . about these smells. I sat down and imagined who these three foreign kings might be.

I couldn't figure it out. There were just too many olfactory anomalies! I got up and walked to the back of whatever this place was to try and collect my thoughts. I felt pleasantly dizzy as I zigzagged beneath the heavenly canopy, inhaling the perfume of the angels and of the centuries to come. The future was dripping with the scent of cinnamon, cloves, and green moss. I could also smell orange and pine.

Fragrances always take us somewhere else, but I needed to come back to the present! I wanted to smell the very heart of this mystery! I walked slowly toward the floral scent of a young woman. A sprinkling of rose and . . . milk . . . aha, she must be a mother, then! The scent that emanated from her was so pure, so moving, that I was tempted to call it the smell of holiness.

Just next to her there was a man who must have been her husband. He smelled strongly of resin and lilies . . . with notes of sawdust and sweat, too. This devoted father must have been running all night. But his worry had been replaced by peace. The couple adored their child.

That was when I then realized that this had all been for him: this child was the reason that the shepherds and kings, the angels and animals, had gathered together tonight. I breathed in his scent and it was . . . divine. The newborn smelled like warm bread. I could see, even now, the grain being ground and the loaves being shared.

Enveloped by the gentle breeze of his spirit, I inhaled . . . again . . . the balm of pure love that was already spreading to the very limits of space and time.

The Broken Santon

Célestin the terracotta figurine looks in sorry shape. The paint on his face is peeling, he is missing part of his knee, and his left hand is broken. He's an old santon who has seen too many Christmases. This year on December first, he was not placed in the nativity scene. Instead, he was thrown straight into the kitchen garbage can.

Sitting amid the trash, Célestin laments:

"I know I look pathetic, and I know I'm no longer worthy of being seen with the angels and shepherds. But I would love to go to the nativity and see Jesus . . . one last time."

The dust bunnies and vegetable peelings in the garbage laugh at him, but he doesn't listen to them. Filled with the hope of Christmas, he pushes and pulls and jiggles until the garbage can at last falls over.

Liberated from his rubbish prison, he jumps for joy and heads for the nativity scene.

After a few days of walking, Célestin is forced to stop. His leg is hurting. The nativity seems so far away. . . . (He still hasn't made it out of the kitchen.) In spite of the pain, the santon limps onward. After an extraordinary effort, he finally arrives in the living room.

Célestin is zigzagging between the toys scattered on the floor when Moustache, the family's cat, suddenly appears. The animal is intrigued by this strange little person and paws at him a few times. Célestin is terrified of the cat's claws and pointy teeth.

"Get out of here, you fat tomcat!" he yells.

But instead of fleeing, the cat grabs the figurine in its mouth, slips out the cat flap, and carries the santon into the backyard. Once Célestin is no longer moving, Moustache no longer finds him the least bit interesting. He abandons him in the middle of a flower bed. At first, the little figurine is relieved to see the feline go. Then he realizes that Moustache has taken him very, very far away from the house and the nativity scene. Célestin is so old, and he feels so tired. He begins to weep with sadness.

That's when he hears someone murmur, "Be strong and have courage. Jesus is waiting for you."

The little santon looks up to see a magnificent flower leaning over him.

"Take one of my petals to dry your tears."

And the pearly flower drops one of its white petals onto Célestin's head.

"Oh, thank you," Célestin says as he wipes his face. "But who are you?"

"I'm the hellebore, but some people also call me the Christmas rose because I bloom in the middle of winter."

"I will never forget your words and kindness."

Célestin feels much better thanks to the hellebore and decides to resume his journey. He travels for entire days between frost-covered blades of grass that look to him like a frozen jungle. He trips and often falls, but he always gets back up. Nothing is stronger than his desire to see Jesus.

In the middle of the yard, Célestin stops
to count the days until Christmas.

There is only one week left before Jesus's birth.

He has to hurry if he wants to arrive in time
and not end up frozen in a pile of dead leaves.

It is very cold. Snow is even starting to fall. It's so pretty!

An enormous snowflake lands near him. Light, white, downy . . . wait . . .
that's not a snowflake! It's a dove! The beautiful bird takes a step back.

"What are you doing out here, little santon?"

"I'm going to the nativity scene to see Jesus."

"But you're so tiny! Climb on my back," the dove offers.

Célestin clutches the dove's neck, and it takes off through the snowflake-filled air. The
bird drops the figurine on a ledge beside the living room window. Célestin turns to say
thank you but it has already flown away into the night.

From where he's standing, Célestin can see the nativity scene and a roaring fire in the
fireplace. He has never felt so close to where he wants to be . . . and so far away. A pane of
glass is separating him from Christmas.

While Célestin shivers in the cold, inside someone places a pretty porcelain plate on the
windowsill. Lounging right in the center of it is a plump gingerbread man. Célestin knocks
on the window to get his attention. With his injured hand, he points to the nativity scene.

The little gingerbread man has only recently come out of the oven. He's quite warm and
is more than happy to open the window for Célestin, who gives him a huge hug to say thank
you. The gingerbread man warms up the santon, and the santon cools down the gingerbread!

"Thank you, gingerbread! You're a great guy! Without you, I might have turned into a snow-covered santon."

"Not a problem! Knock and the door shall be opened—who was it who said that again?"

"Jesus! As a matter of fact, that's who I'm on my way to see now."

"Happy trails! I'm staying here. I'm too afraid of being eaten by the cat!"

Célestin waves goodbye to the gingerbread man and slides down the curtain onto the soft living room rug. When he sees Moustache, he decides to hide under the rug's tassels and immediately falls asleep.

The next day, after hobbling along for a few hours, Célestin finally reaches the sideboard where the nativity scene is displayed. For a moment, the piece of furniture seems impossible to climb. But the figurine has faith, a faith that can move mountains!

He gathers the last of his strength and climbs up the Christmas tree next to the sideboard. He pulls himself from branch to branch until he has reached the star on the top, which happens to be at the same height as the nativity scene. From there, he throws himself onto the sideboard table.

He lands on a clump of moss in the middle of some sheep, exhausted but happy!

For all of Advent, the courageous little santon has been walking toward Jesus in spite of all of his doubts and obstacles. He has finally reached him, just in time for Christmas!

More delighted than ever to see the nativity, Célestin stands himself in the back row of santons behind the fishmonger and the knife-grinder. He doesn't want to be noticed and tossed into the garbage can again . . . and he doesn't feel like he deserves to be in the front row, anyway.

He says a simple prayer with his half-painted smile:

"Jesus, I offer you all of my wounds and the long path I have taken to reach you!"

Then the angels take Célestin by the hand and gently move aside the other little terracotta figurines so the broken santon can see the child of God.

Face to face with Jesus, Célestin closes his eyes with happiness.

He is in heaven.